CIVIL WAR VICTORY AND THE COSTLY AFTERMATH

THE CIVIL WAR

CIVIL WAR VICTORY AND THE COSTLY AFTERMATH

MASON CREST

Mason Crest
450 Parkway Drive, Suite D
Broomall, PA 19008
www.masoncrest.com

Printed and bound in the United States of America.

First printing
9 8 7 6 5 4 3 2 1

ISBN: 978-1-4222-3886-8
Series ISBN: 978-1-4222-3881-3
ebook ISBN: 978-1-4222-7896-3
ebook series ISBN: 978-1-4222-7891-8

Produced by Regency House Publishing Limited
The Manor House
High Street
Buntingford
Hertfordshire
SG9 9AB
United Kingdom

www.regencyhousepublishing.com

Text copyright © 2018 Regency House Publishing Limited/Jonathan Sutherland and
Diane Canwell

PAGE 2: Arlington Memorial Bridge in Washington, DC.

PAGE 3: Lee's surrender 1865. "Peace in Union"
The surrender of General Lee to General Grant at Appomattox Court House, Virginia, April 9, 1865.

RIGHT: Ulysses S. Grant.

PAGE 6: Gettysburg Cemetery. Headstones of soldiers from the American military at the site of the American Civil War at Gettysburg, Pennsylvania.

CONTENTS

KEY ICONS TO LOOK FOR:

Words to Understand: These words with their easy-to-understand definitions will increase the reader's understanding of the text, while building vocabulary skills.

Sidebars: This boxed material within the main text allows readers to build knowledge, gain insights, explore possibilities, and broaden their perspectives by weaving together additional information to provide realistic and holistic perspectives.

Educational Videos: Readers can view videos by scanning our QR codes, providing them with additional content to supplement the text. Examples include news coverage, moments in history, speeches, iconic sports moments, and much more!

Text-Dependent Questions: These questions send the reader back to the text for more careful attention to the evidence presented here.

Research Projects: Readers are pointed toward areas of further inquiry connected to each chapter. Suggestions are provided for projects that encourage deeper research and analysis.

Series Glossary of Key Terms: This back-of-the-book glossary contains terminology used throughout the series. Words found here increase the reader's ability to read and comprehend high-level books and articles in this field.

General Robert E. Lee with son Custis (left) and aide Walter H. Taylor (right).

Lincoln Memorial

The grand Lincoln Memorial is an American national monument built to honor the 16th President of the United States, Abraham Lincoln. It was designed by Henry Bacon, a New York architect. He had spent time studying in Europe where he was influenced and inspired by ancient Greek architecture. It was based on the architecture of a Greek temple. There are 36 Doric columns, each one representing one state of the U.S. at the date of President Lincoln's death.

The memorial contains a large seated sculpture of Abraham Lincoln. The nineteen-foot tall statue of Abraham Lincoln was designed by Daniel Chester French who was a leading sculptor from Massachusetts. The marble statue was carved in white Georgia marble by the Piccirilli brothers. The interior murals were painted by Jules Guerin. Ernest C. Bairstow created the exterior details with carvings by Evelyn Beatrice Longman. The memorial is inscribed with Lincoln's famous speech, "The Gettysburg Address." The words of the speech are etched into the wall to inspire all Americans just as it did in 1863. To the right is the entire Second Inaugural Address, given by Lincoln in March 1865. The memorial itself is 190 feet long, 119 feet wide, and almost 100 feet high. It took 8 years to complete from 1914–1922.

At its most basic level the Lincoln Memorial symbolizes the idea of Freedom. The Lincoln Memorial is often used as a gathering place for protests and political rallies. The Memorial has become a symbolically sacred venue especially for the Civil Rights movement. On August 28, 1963, the memorial grounds were the site of the *March on Washington for Jobs and Freedom*, which proved to the high point of the *American Civil Rights Movement*. It is estimated that approximately 250,000 people came to the event, where they heard Martin Luther King, Jr. deliver his historic speech *"I have a Dream."* King's speech, with its language of patriotism and its evocation of Lincoln's Gettysburg Address, was meant to match the symbolism of the Lincoln Memorial as a monument to national unity.

The Lincoln Memorial is located on the western end of the National Mall in Washington, D.C., across from the Washington Monument, and towers over the Reflecting Pool. The memorial is maintained by the U.S. National Park Service, and receives approximately 8 million visitors each year. It is open 24 hours a day and is free to all visitors.

Chapter One
THE ROAD TO VICTORY

With all the activity, maneuvering and fighting taking place in the East, it is easy to forget that there was also a war going on in the West. On June 9, 1862 Union General Buell took control of the Army of the Ohio, aiming to tackle Confederate troops in East Tennessee. The first target was to be Chattanooga, though there was a problem in that the Confederate cavalry, under the command of

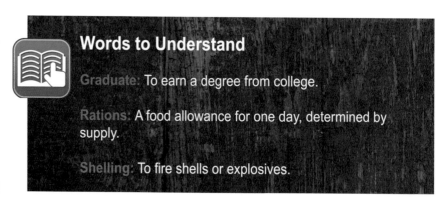

Words to Understand

Graduate: To earn a degree from college.

Rations: A food allowance for one day, determined by supply.

Shelling: To fire shells or explosives.

OPPOSITE: Battle of Lookout Mountain, November 24, 1863, Army of the Cumberland
Lithograph by Kurz & Allison, ca.1889.

RIGHT: Men repairing a single-track railroad after the Battle of Stone's River, Murfreesboro, December 31, 1862–January 2, 1863.

Forrest and Morgan, was continually raiding the area through which he needed to pass. These raiders regularly attacked Union outposts, bridges, and supply columns.

On August 30, 1862 Union troops advanced against Richmond, Kentucky. Many of the Northern soldiers were raw recruits and it was an unmitigated disaster, with nearly 1,000 killed or wounded and over 4,500 captured.

Focus then switched to the Cumberland Gap, which was something of a gateway into East Tennessee. Union troops were stationed there by the end of August, in the hope that Morgan's supplies would be cut off. The Confederate troops tried to dislodge them and a concerted effort was made on September 17. This time the Union troops withdrew and on October 3 reached the Ohio river.

While the Confederates were threatening the Cumberland Gap, Confederate Generals Bragg and Kirby-Smith decided to launch a campaign against Buell, who had concentrated his troops at Nashville. When he heard the Confederates were heading in his direction, he left a holding force at Nashville and took the bulk of his army to Bowling Green. After achieving a victory at Munfordville, the Confederates issued a proclamation to Kentucky, asking it to support the Confederacy, and a provisional governor was inaugurated on October 4.

After the Confederate army, under Van Dorn, had been defeated at Corinth, Mississippi, on October 4, Bragg found himself pretty much on his own. Bragg's main army was at Louisville and Buell made several diversionary attacks, which culminated in an inconclusive engagement at Perryville on October 8. After this, Bragg's army moved to Murfreesboro, Tennessee, in what was effectively a retreat, destroying any supplies that could not be

ABOVE LEFT: General George W. Morgan.

ABOVE CENTER: General James Longstreet.

ABOVE: General Edmund Kirby-Smith.

LEFT: General Buell.

OPPOSITE: Topographical Sketch of the Battlefield of Stone (Stones) River Drawn by Lt. O.R. Dahl, 2nd Brigade, 1st Division, 1862.

carried. Buell gave chase and the cavalry clashed 26 times along the route.

Buell's reluctance to close with the Confederates again angered Washington and he was relieved of his command. William Rosecrans, who assumed command of the Army of the Cumberland, as the force was now known, replaced him on October 20.

On December 26 Rosecrans finally ordered the army to march on Murfreesboro, but it was continually harassed by Confederate cavalry as it advanced. The first main engagement took place on December 30, 1862, but both sides were content to fire artillery at one another. The following day, the two armies were quiet and the Confederates believed that Rosecrans was about to retreat. To their horror, however, the Confederates discovered that the Union force had taken the opportunity to dig in, and the Confederates were forced to drive the Union troops out of their entrenchments. But the assault was disastrous and cost the Confederate army over 10,000 casualties out of its total force of 40,000. Bragg retreated and Rosecrans entered Murfreesboro.

Bragg's army had simply not been strong enough to deal with Rosecrans' force, which in this campaign had amounted to some 43,000. After some wrangling, General Longstreet's corps of the Army of Northern Virginia was sent to reinforce Bragg, but failed to reach him before another major battle took place. Bragg had established his base at Chattanooga by July 1863, but by early September he realized how dangerous his position was, with a Union army of some 57,000 bearing down on him.

On the morning of September 19, Union troops were approaching Chickamauga. There was a skirmish between dismounted cavalry to begin with, but both sides began to reinforce. When the general engagement took place the following day, September 20, the Confederates took the offensive. The Union left was thrown into confusion and reinforcements did not reach the front in time. By this stage Longstreet's troops had arrived and he was thrown into the battle, hitting the Union right. The Union troops held and both sides were badly mauled. With great reluctance Rosecrans ordered his army to withdraw from what had been a bloody engagement. Rosecrans had deployed 58,000 men and had suffered over 16,000 casualties, while the Confederates, including Longstreet, had some 66,000 men engaged and had lost nearly 18,500.

It now seemed that the Confederacy was about to sweep the Union forces out of Tennessee, and desperate action was needed. Troops were detached from the Army of the Potomac, but it was necessary for them to travel on over 1,100 miles (1770km) of connecting railroad lines.

RIGHT: Chickamauga Battlefield Drawn by J.C. McElroy, ca.1895.

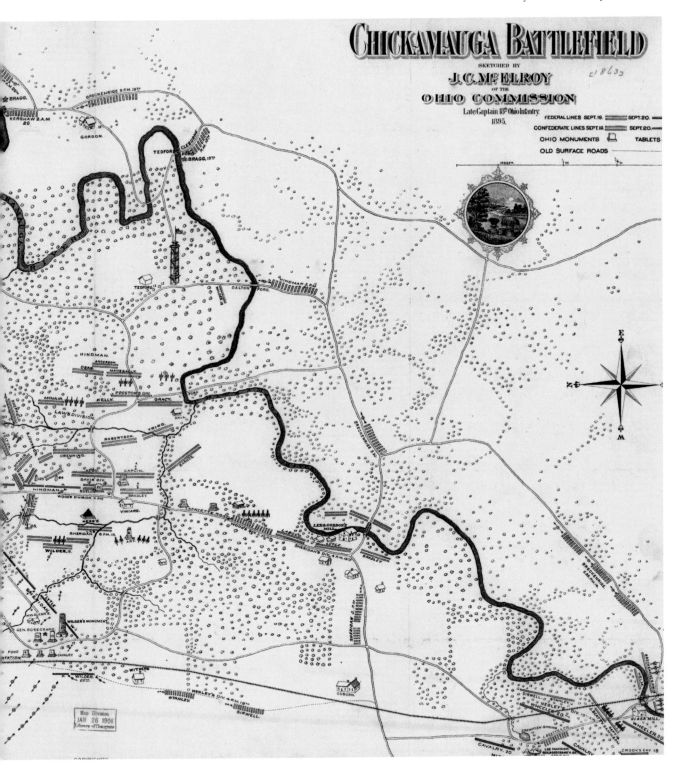

Some of the units got there by September 30, but others did not arrive until October 16, the day on which Grant was given command of the Military Division of the Mississippi. This would incorporate the departments of the Ohio, the Cumberland, the Tennessee, and responsibilities in Mississippi.

One of Grant's first actions was to ensure his supply lines were properly protected. Having established his main base at Chattanooga, on a bend of the Tennessee river, he could now be assured that by using the river as the main supply

OPPOSITE: William Tecumseh Sherman.

ABOVE: General Braxton Bragg.

MAJOR GENERAL WILLIAM STARKE ROSECRANS (1819–1898)

William Starke Rosecrans was born in Little Taylor Run, Ohio on September 6, 1819 to Crandall Rosecrans and Jemima Hopkins. He received little formal education and was largely self-taught by reading. He entered West Point in 1838 where he excelled in his studies. During the Civil War he became famous for his successes, becoming the victor at prominent Western Theater battles. However, his military career was effectively ended following his catastrophic defeat at the Battle of Chickamauga in 1863. In 1864 he became involved in politics and was briefly considered as a vice presidential running mate for Lincoln. After the war he was appointed several political and diplomatic positions and in 1880 was elected to Congress as a Democratic representative for California.

Rosencrans was also an accomplised businessman, becoming involved in a multitude of businesses. In February 1898 Rosecrans's health deteriorated rapidly following a bout of pneumonia. This was worsend when one of his favorite grandchildren died of diphtheria. Rosecrans was seized with grief and died in March 1989. Even after death his name lives on with Fort Rosecrans National Cemetery being named after him in his honor, along with a street in Los Angeles.

line, his troops would be adequately fed and equipped.

The Confederates, meanwhile, keeping a close eye on the Union force, had established positions on high ground around Chattanooga. Their positions ran from the East Tennessee & Georgia Railroad in the north, along Missionary Ridge to Rossville, and additional forces were posted on Lookout Mountain to the south-west of Chattanooga. With more troops still arriving, Grant determined to dislodge the Confederate army.

At 1540 on November 24 signal guns were fired and nearly 25,000 Union troops rushed forward to storm Confederate positions along Missionary Ridge. The assault was so overwhelming that the Confederates, after firing a few shots, fell back in disorder. Bragg ordered his troops to fall back to Chickamauga.

Grant had discovered on November 4 that Longstreet had moved towards Knoxville to threaten General Burnside's Union army. In order to force Longstreet to return to the front near Chattanooga, Grant determined to launch an assault. Burnside's forces were well dug in and it would not be an easy task to dislodge him. The assaults against Burnside were timed for November 28, but bad weather put the engagement back a day. No sooner had Longstreet's men been

RIGHT: General Grant Looking over the Battlefield at Fort Donelson, ca.1863.
Paul Phillipoteaux (1846–1923).
Oil on canvas.

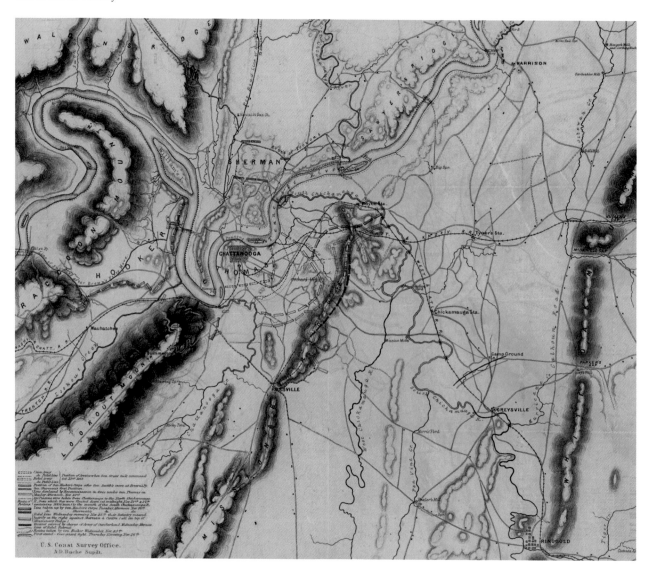

committed, than a telegram arrived telling him to return immediately to support Bragg, with the result that the siege against Burnside was broken almost as soon as it had begun.

Soon after, Longstreet rejoined the Army of Northern Virginia. General Polk replaced Bragg, but on December 27 Polk, in turn, was replaced by General Joseph E. Johnston. Things were not going all that well for the Union army during the winter of 1863/64. Sherman, in command of the Department of the Tennessee, was still suffering attacks from roving bands of Confederate raiders, and decided to raise a large cavalry force and attack Meridian. The attack got under way on February 3, 1864, with the cavalry covering 150 miles (240km) in 11 days. Everything that Sherman's cavalry could

ABOVE: Sketch of the Battles of Chattanooga, November 23–26, 1863.

OPPOSITE ABOVE: Blockhouse on the Nashville & Chattanooga Railroad during the Battle of Chattanooga.

OPPOSITE BELOW: Confederate prisoners, Chattanooga.

not take with them they destroyed, including railroads.

On March 2, 1864 General Grant was given overall command of the Union armies, in the hope that he would co-ordinate the Union effort. After reorganizing the Union armies, Grant began to frame the strategy by which the Confederacy would be defeated. Sherman's force amounted to nearly 99,000 men and he would attack Johnston. Thomas had over 60,000 men in Chattanooga, McPherson had 25,000 in Huntsville, Alabama, and Schofield had 13,500 in Knoxville, Tennessee. Facing them were just 50,000 Confederates under Johnston. Sherman launched his Georgia campaign on May 5, 1864. There was heavy fighting and very soon the Confederates were in full retreat.

Johnston eventually fell back to New Hope, where he amassed 64,000 men. The Confederates were occupying three prominent hills: Kennesaw, Pine Mountain, and Lost Mountain. Sherman's armies moved up to engage. After dreadful weather it was finally decided that the Union troops would assault the Confederate line on June 27, 1864, with attacks coming in along the entire 10-mile (16-km) front. This had mixed results and in some places ground was taken, but losses were high. When the Union army threatened his flank a few days later, Johnston withdrew from Kennesaw.

Sherman ordered his cavalry to strike deep behind Confederate lines and into Alabama, before beginning his advance towards Atlanta. Johnston was unsure what to do, and General Hood replaced him on July 17. Hood had acquired an army in fairly poor condition and it had

lost nearly a third of its strength, there being a mere 49,000 men when Hood became commander. Hood was determined to defend Atlanta and saw his opportunity on 20 July, as Union troops pushed forward. They clashed at Peachtree Creek, but the Confederates were no match for the strong Union force. Hood pulled out of contact and the Union army moved on, ever closer to Atlanta.

Despite bitter counter-offensives, Sherman's army was just 20 miles (32km) south of Atlanta by September 2, 1864. Hood had decided to abandon the city for fear of being surrounded. He decided to attempt to draw Sherman back towards the

OPPOSITE ABOVE: Chattanooga from the north.

ABOVE: Lieutenant General Jubal Early.

OPPOSITE BELOW and RIGHT: Umbrella Rock on Lookout Mountain, Chattanooga, Tennessee.

mountains and there, in restricted ground, to defeat him.

By October 1 Hood was heading for Nashville, by which stage he had around 40,000 men and was being pursued by 60,000 under Sherman. It was then learned that Hood had surrounded the Federal supply base at Allatoona, held by fewer than 900 men. The attack failed and Hood

broke off, believing that a large Union force was close by.

Sherman now decided to force Hood to face him. He would march across Georgia and head for Savannah and Charleston and Hood would have to follow. By October 31 Hood had reached Tuscumbia, Alabama, but it had been left to General Thomas to deal with Hood,

ABOVE: Scouts and guides of the Army of the Potomac at Brandy Station, Virginia, March 1864.

LEFT: U.S. Military Telegraph battery wagon, Army of the Potomac, Petersburg, Virginia, 1864.

OPPOSITE ABOVE: Lt. General Leonidas Polk, officer of the Confederate army.

OPPOSITE BELOW: Battle of Missionary Ridge, November 25, 1863 Chromolithograph, Cosack & Co., ca.1886.

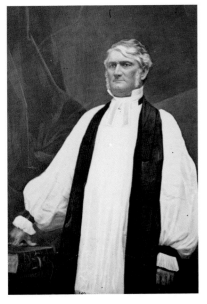

because by November 10 Sherman was on his way to bring devastation to the heart of the Confederacy.

Meanwhile, in the East, the Army of the Potomac had reorganized, having been strengthened over the winter of 1863/64. On May 4 1864, under the direct command of Grant and ably assisted by Meade, it was determined to launch a major offensive. Throughout the winter, Lee had been settled around the Fredericksburg and Chancellorsville area. He could call on some 62,000 men, whereas Grant and Meade had 118,000 at their disposal.

Lead elements of the Union army attacked Confederate outposts close to the

Rapidan river on May 4. The main army crossed the following day and headquarters were set up at the Wilderness Tavern. Lee could not afford to engage until Longstreet's force rejoined him on May 6, but Grant was already pushing cavalry forward and it now seemed certain there would be a battle. Grant was aware that Longstreet was due to arrive with 12,000 reinforcements.

On May 6, at 5:00am, the Union army attacked in force, the blow falling on Major General Wilcox's division. The Confederates began to fall back, with Lee desperately hoping that Longstreet would arrive. Eventually Longstreet did

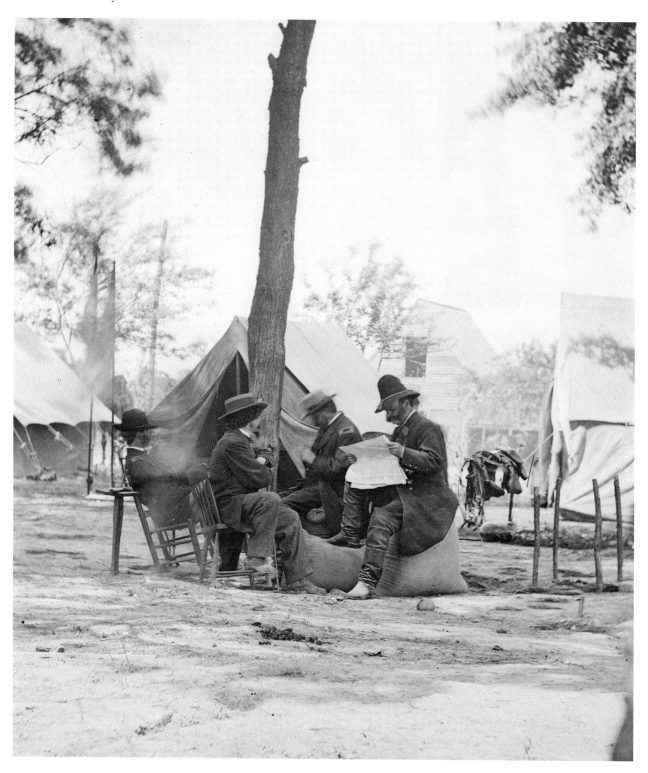

arrive, halted the Confederate retreat and began to push the Union army back. Unfortunately, Longstreet was hit by a bullet, causing severe bleeding. That night the pinewoods of the Wilderness caught fire due to the **shelling** and many men were burned to death.

On the morning of May 7, Grant planned to head south-east towards

OPPOSITE: General Burnside (reading newpaper) with Mathew B. Brady (nearest tree) at the Army of the Potomac headquarters (possibly at Cold Harbor, Virginia).

ABOVE: Kennesaw Mountain.

RIGHT: Spotsylvania Courthouse.

Spotsylvania Courthouse. Grant had seen the danger as a smaller Union force, under Butler, had landed at City Point on May 5, and that Lee could swiftly move towards Richmond and destroy Butler's force. Lee had ordered elements of his army to head for Spotsylvania, but this was delayed due to the forest fires and the fact that Union cavalry was engaged at Todd's Tavern, close by.

Sheridan, at the head of the Union cavalry, planned a raid on Richmond,

BELOW LEFT: General George H. Thomas.

BELOW: General Ambrose Burnside.

OPPOSITE ABOVE: Sketch showing positions and entrenchments of the Army of North Virginia during the battles for Spotsylvania Courthouse from May 9–21, 1864.

OPPOSITE BELOW: Maj. General George G. Meade, officer of the Federal army, with corps commanders, June 1865.

beginning on May 9, 1864, and he would be absent for 16 days. Confederate trains were intercepted and Union prisoners freed, and warehouses containing **rations** for the army were destroyed. Eventually J.E.B. Stuart's cavalry caught up with Sheridan and there were running skirmishes from May 10. Stuart's cavalry reached Yellow Tavern before Sheridan, taking up defensive positions around the Telegraph Road, and at around 4:00pm on May 11 Sheridan's cavalry arrived. It managed to drive back Stuart's left; Stuart rushed to rally his men and in the confusing fight an unhorsed Union trooper saw a mounted Confederate officer to his side. He fired his pistol, hitting Stuart, who died the following day. He had **graduated** from West Point in 1854 and was only 31 years old.

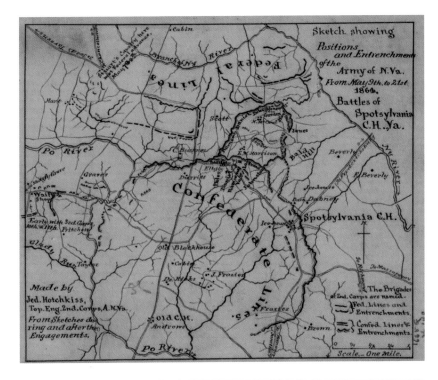

Meanwhile the Confederates had taken up positions on high ground around Spotsylvania, arranging themselves in a semi-circle, with Spotsylvania Courthouse within the 3-mile (5-km) defensive line. Lee's troops had been digging in from the evening of May 8, felling trees and piling up earthworks; part of the defensive works would become known as Bloody Angle. This was a salient point in the Confederate line held by men from Ewell's corps. The fighting was so frenzied in that area that the ground was soon covered with layer upon layer of bodies. Grant fanatically pushed his men forward, regardless of casualties, and at around midnight on May 12 the Confederate army withdrew. Grant had lost nearly 13,500 men and the Confederates around 10,000.

There were five days of continual rain after Spotsylvania, and the news for the Union was not good. Union troops had been defeated at Newmarket, at Drewry's Bluff, and in Louisiana. On May 19 Grant

OPPOSITE ABOVE LEFT: General Matthew Butler, Confederate army.

OPPOSITE ABOVE RIGHT: General Sheridan (right), General Katz (seated) and a friend.

OPPOSITE BELOW: General Cadmus Wilcox of the Confederate army.

ABOVE: Allatoona Pass, Georgia, looking north.

decided to make his new base at Port Royal, on the Rappahannock, but on the same day Lee was on the offensive, attacking 6,000 untried Union troops under General Taylor. Fortunately, the Union troops were able to hold out.

On May 20 Grant took the initiative, though he was taking a chance in splitting up his corps, and moved towards Richmond, taking the route from Guiney's

Station to Bowling Green, then Milford. The armies clashed at North Anna Bridge on the evening of May 23 and once again the Confederates were thrown back. By now Grant was certain Lee was in difficulties and told Washington: "Lee is really whipped. The prisoners we now take show it, and the action of his army shows it unmistakeably. I may be mistaken, but I feel that our success over Lee's army is already assured." Grant could not have been more wrong.

By the morning of May 27 Sheridan's cavalry had reached Hanover Ferry. This allowed the Union army to cross the Pamunkey the following day. Lee was determined to prevent Grant from finding an open road to Richmond. He was asking Richmond for more troops and was determined that Grant should not reach the Chickahominy river. Lee wanted General Beauregard to join him in his efforts to crush Grant, but Beauregard was of the opinion that Lee should be defending along the Chickahominy and that he should be sending troops to him.

BELOW: Port Royal on the Rappahannock river, during Grant's Wilderness Campaign.

OPPOSITE: Drewry's Bluff, on the James river, where the battle took place in May 1862.

PIERRE GUSTAVE TOUTANT BEAUREGARD (1818–1893)

Born in Louisiana, Beauregard attended West Point in 1838, graduating second in his class and acquiring the nickname "The Little Napoleon." By 1861 he had been made superintendent at West Point, but resigned his commission to become a brigadier general in the Confederate army, and it was Beauregard's troops who attacked and took Fort Sumter. He took tactical command at the First Bull Run, and is credited with drafting the attack orders for the Battle of Shiloh. After he was forced to evacuate his supply base in Mississippi, he was relieved of his command in June 1862, returning to lead the Confederates in the Carolinas. Beauregard's greatest victory was at Drewry's Bluff against Benjamin Butler. He managed to ward off Union attempts to take Petersburg while Robert E. Lee was positioned north of the James river. In September 1864 Beauregard returned to the Western theater and operated with Hood and Taylor, but they were unsuccessful in preventing Sherman from marching to the sea. When the war ended, Beauregard refused offers of a command abroad. He was involved in railroads and became Louisiana's Adjutant General. He died on February 20, 1893 and was buried at Metairie, Louisiana.

On May 15 Lee had learned from a captured despatch that upwards of 25,000 new Union troops were en route to Grant from Washington. Beauregard and Lee met together on May 29, the upshot being that Lee would engage Grant with whatever troops he had. On May 30 Sheridan's cavalry managed to move towards Hanover Courthouse, where Confederate cavalry was encountered. Sheridan was able to overrun the Confederate defenses, losing 228 men in the process, while the Confederates lost around 450.

At 1700 on the same day, Lieutenant General Jubal Early, who had succeeded Ewell, attacked the Union left, and additional reinforcements were required to push the Confederates off. On the same afternoon there was further cavalry action near Old Church and the Confederate cavalry was pushed back towards Cold Harbor. On May 31 Sheridan attacked Confederate cavalry under General Fitzhugh Lee, close to the crossroads at Cold Harbor. The Confederates were pushed back for some distance and Sheridan held the ground.

It was now clear that Grant was advancing towards Cold Harbor. Lee immediately seized the chance to turn Grant's flank and moved troops out of his main front line, placing them a mile to the north-west of Cold Harbor. Awaiting the

LEFT: The 12th Pennsylvania Volunteers at Bloody Angle.

OPPOSITE: A party of the 50th New York Engineers engaged in road-building along the banks of the North Anna river.

Union thrust were around 15,000 Confederates. The Confederates attacked at dawn on June 1, but met with almost immediate disaster. Lawrence Keitt, leading the attack and riding at the head of his brigade, was shot within minutes and his regiment broke for cover.

Things were shaping up for a major confrontation. Lee expected Grant to attack in force on June 2, but the attack had been pushed back to 4:30am on June 3. This would be the principal action in the Battle of Cold Harbor and would turn out to be the single most expensive assault in

terms of casualties that the Union army had ever launched. Three corps were moving forward to take part in the attack, but during the night it had rained and the ground was muddy. It was also difficult for the corps to keep in touch with one another due to the contours of the terrain. No

sooner had the Union troops come into view than they were subjected to fire. In General Hancock's 2nd Corps no fewer than eight colonels died in the first assault alone, each of the corps commanders having been told to attack with their entire force. It was an unmitigated disaster and in just half an hour Grant's army suffered 7,000 casualties. By 7:30am the battle was over. Reluctantly Grant called it a day at 12:00pm.

An unfortunate incident occurred between Grant and Lee after the battle of Cold Harbor, when time was wasted while the two wrangled over a cease-fire that would allow their wounded to be gathered up. Despite men left groaning on the battlefield, neither would concede the terms

OPPOSITE: Drewry's Bluff, interior of the Confederate Fort Darling.

ABOVE: Hanover Courthouse, Virginia.

RIGHT: The Peninsula Campaign, May–August 1862: a Howitzer gun is captured by Butterfield's brigade near Hanover Courthouse.

of the cease-fire, and it took 48 hours for them to finally agree, by which time hundreds of men, left lying in the mud, had died from their wounds.

It seems that Lee was the more pleased with the results of the battle. He

wrote to the Confederate Secretary of War: "So far every attack of the enemy has been repulsed. Repeated attacks were made. They were met with great steadiness and repulsed in every instance. The attack extended to our extreme left, under General Early, with like results. Later in the day it was twice renewed against General Heth but was repulsed with loss. Our loss today has been small, and our success, under the blessing of God, all that we could expect." Indeed, Lee's force had probably lost 1,200 killed and wounded against at least 11,000 Union casualties.

So far the Wilderness Campaign, with its huge death toll, had been too costly. The only thing that gave comfort to the Union, at this time, was the persistent progress of Sherman, who was steadily marching

number). Harper's Ferry was abandoned and 5,000 men, under General Sigel, crossed the Potomac river and occupied the Maryland Heights, joined by the troops that had evacuated Harper's Ferry.

By July 6 Early was in Sharpsburg, where an opportunity had arisen. There were 17,000 Confederate prisoners-of-war at Point Lookout at the tip of Maryland, just at the point where the Potomac flows

LEFT: General Fitzhugh Lee.

ABOVE: General Winfield Scott Hancock.

OPPOSITE: The Chickahominy river.

towards the sea and the Carolinas. It was difficult to maintain morale, but Grant's army, despite the losses, was still growing.

Lee feared Grant would now move against Petersburg, but in the meantime he had some breathing space and sent Jubal Early from Gaines' Mill into the Shenandoah Valley. It was a diversionary attack: he knew that Early could deal with the Union troops under General Hunter in the Shenandoah Valley and after that he would be able to cross the Potomac and threaten Washington.

Waves of panic struck the Union ranks in the belief that Early was at the head of 20,000 men (it was in fact half that into Chesapeake Bay. The operation to free the prisoners was being controlled by Colonel John Taylor Wood, who proposed to attack the camp using gunboats, before linking up with Early close to Baltimore. The 17,000 men could then join Early's army. The plan, however, was abandoned as the Confederates learned the Union government had been

removing the prisoners from Point Lookout since June 10.

Early presented a considerable problem. He was marching towards the Potomac, but the garrison defenses surrounding Washington consisted of fewer than 10,000 men, while some 53 forts, over a perimeter of 37 miles (59km), surrounded the city itself. Each of the forts

had a liberal allocation of artillery pieces, but they would need 25,000 infantry, 9,000 artillerymen and around 3,000 cavalry to man them all.

Grant was ordered to send men back to Washington, beginning with over 2,000 men, followed by additional divisions. Troops were rushed from Baltimore and by July 7 detachments of the Army of the

Potomac, sent by Grant, had arrived in Baltimore. As Early approached the Monocacy river on Saturday July 9, 1864 he encountered Union troops waiting for him on the east bank. After a full day's fighting, the Confederates forced the Union contingent of around 6,000 back, leaving the road to Washington open, there being no major Union formations between the Confederate army and the capital. There was understandable panic.

Early continued towards Washington, sending advance units down the Georgetown Pike, while his main force moved from Rockville towards Silver Spring. He was on the road to Seventh Street Pike, a main road leading directly into Washington. Near Silver Spring, Early was delayed by a small detachment of Union cavalry, but shortly after midday he was in sight of Fort Stevens, where he rested. He noted the defensive positions

were barely manned, but suddenly there was dust on the horizon, from which a column of Union infantry emerged; Union artillery batteries began to open fire on the Confederates. Early had around 8,000 infantry and 40 artillery pieces, and if he was to move on Washington he would have to be quick.

As the hours passed, more Union troops took up positions in the fort and the defense works around the Georgetown

Pike. Early was concerned that if he gave battle now, and lost, his men would be trapped; Union forces were undoubtedly in

OPPOSITE: A cooking tent at Fredericksburg during the Wilderness Campaign.

ABOVE: Soldiers filling canteens at Fredericksburg during the Wilderness Campaign.

possession of the passes around South Mountain and were covering the fords of the Upper Potomac. As the day drew on, even more Union troops began to arrive, some on steamers. Perhaps Early's chance to catch Washington unawares had been lost, but he was determined to assault the fortifications on July 12.

The defense of Fort Stevens was witnessed by no other than President Lincoln himself. Union forces were now

strong enough to deal with Early on the open field, but still Early held back, concerned that his men would be slaughtered. Finally it was the Union forces that prompted action by opening fire with artillery at 6:00pm. Union infantry moved forward, but met with determined resistance, and after taking nearly 300 casualties the Union troops withdrew, back to their defense works. Early knew full well that his opportunity

had been lost and made plans to withdraw. He left just 200 men behind to act as a rearguard and his footsore men began to fall back through Rockville to Poolesville before crossing the Potomac river at White's Ford on July 14. He allowed his men to rest at Leesburg, then headed into the Shenandoah Valley.

The Shenandoah Valley had been of importance during the entire war, being the place where General Stonewall Jackson made his name, having beaten and confounded far larger Union forces with a relatively small force throughout late 1861 and into 1862. The Shenandoah Valley was no less important by 1864, but this time the

ABOVE: Federal Generals Hancock (seated), Gibbon, Barlow, and Birney.

OPPOSITE: The site after the Battle of Cold Harbor.

situation had been reversed, and considerable numbers of Union troops were operating in the Shenandoah Valley. On May 15, 1864 there had been a battle at Newmarket, which the Confederates had won, but it had not stopped the Union army from destroying houses, factories, and mills.

It was decided that a Confederate force would enter Pennsylvania and collect $100,000 in gold as payment for the damage done in the Shenandoah. A Confederate force of only a brigade, under Brigadier General McCausland, crossed the River Potomac on July 29. He made for Chambersburg and when the Union inhabitants refused to pay he burned the place to the ground. On his return to Virginia, McCausland was intercepted at Moorfield, West Virginia, on August 7, losing 500 men at a minimal cost to the Union force.

On August 11 Union cavalry, under General George Custer, attacked Early's troops 3 miles (5km) from Winchester, forcing them back, and there was another sharp fight close to Strasburg the following day. Confederate cavalry raided Union supply trains on August 13 and due to this and many other problems the Union troops fell back to Charlestown.

The Union army, now under the command of Major General Sheridan, went back on the offensive in early September, reaching Berryville on September 3, where it dug in. The Confederates were driven out of Martinsburg on September 18 and there was another fight at Winchester the next day, the Confederates being forced back each time. By September 20 the Union army had reoccupied the defensive

the battlefield at 10:30am, with an army that seemed on the verge of collapse, though his presence brought fresh hope. Even though the Union camp had been overrun by Confederates, who had grabbed equipment and food, which they had not seen for some months, Sheridan organized attacks and eventually his infantry began

to advance once again. Early pulled away but many of his men were caught, overburdened with loot, though he eventually established a new line 7 miles (11km) below Mount Jackson. There were several other small battles, but this was the last major engagement in the 1864 Shenandoah Valley Campaign.

positions that it had held before along Cedar Creek.

The main Confederate position was on Fishers Hill, which Union troops stormed at dawn on September 22. Having taken heavy casualties, Early's Confederates began to retire towards Charlottesville, and with the exception of Confederate raiding and some cavalry clashes, all was quiet until mid-October.

It was now October 19 and Sheridan had been to Washington. He was returning to Winchester when, at 6:00am, he received intelligence that there was firing in the direction of his forces. In what was later known as Sheridan's Ride, he proceeded cross-country to avoid roads and wounded men. Indeed, his army was engaged against Early's Confederates. Sheridan arrived on

OPPOSITE LEFT: Major General Franz Sigel.

OPPOSITE RIGHT: Major General Philip H. Sheridan.

ABOVE: Gaines' Mill in ruins.

During the campaign Union casualties had been close on 17,000, while Confederate casualties are difficult to assess, but at Cedar Creek alone the Confederates lost close on 3,000 men.

The struggle for Tennessee was about to intensify. Sherman had already left the area and was marching through Georgia. This left almost 60,000 Union troops, under Major General Thomas, in Tennessee, while General Hood, who determined to launch a new campaign in Tennessee and destroy Thomas's army, commanded the Confederates. The campaign got under way on November 19, 1864, with Hood's troops reaching Columbia on the Duck river on November 27. Union troops at Pulaski withdrew to Nashville, while more Union troops headed

for Columbia to dig in before Hood arrived. As Hood approached and tried to get round Columbia, the Union troops, under Schofield, also pulled back.

Hood advanced towards Franklin, where he encountered more Union troops. There was a sharp fight, which inflicted relatively heavy casualties on the Confederates, and Hood's army was significantly weakened by this engagement and the arrival of more Union troops. Grant, Lincoln and others now realized there was a golden opportunity to destroy the Confederate Army of Tennessee, but

Thomas was not yet ready to launch a major offensive. He was waiting for additional cavalry and Grant eventually lost his patience and decided to replace Thomas with Schofield on December 9. As it was, the Battle of Nashville took place between December 15 and 16, 1864. Union troops amounted to some 55,000, with Hood's strength a little under 38,000.

The Union army advanced to push the Confederates out of their entrenchments around Nashville, pushing them back a short distance on the first day. Fighting continued into December 16 and this time determined attacks broke through and made Hood's positions untenable, completing the disintegration of Hood's army. Thomas, still in charge, as Schofield had not yet replaced him, took over 13,000 Confederate prisoners. Hood resigned his command but was ordered to Texas to organize troops. He would eventually turn himself into the Union army in late May 1865.

Sherman's famous March to the Sea occurred in the fall of 1864 when, with around 60,000 troops at his disposal, he marched from Kingston to Savannah, a distance of over 300 miles (480km), between November 12 and December 22, 1864. During the march he destroyed factories, stores, mills, in fact anything he

LEFT: Sheridan's Famous Ride at the Battle of Cedar Creek, Virginia, in 1864 Thure de Thulstrup (1848–1930). Chromolithograph.

thought would support the Confederate armies. His troops occupied Savannah on December 22, where he received reinforcements, men being now available following the destruction of Hood's army. Sherman's march caused a great outcry at the time and has been much criticized over the years for its destructive nature. Between November 14 and 16 Sherman's army destroyed much of Atlanta, leaving the city in flames.

The Confederates were almost completely powerless to stop Sherman, and all that could be scraped together were around 10,000 regular troops to protect Savannah. In fact Sherman did not meet with any real opposition until he was almost at Savannah, where the Confederates had thrown up some fortifications, but were quickly carried at bayonet point. The Confederates in Savannah, under General Hardee, abandoned the city on December 20, and

having reached his goal, Sherman was then ordered to turn north to cut off Confederate troops from joining Lee's Army of Northern Virginia. Consequently, Sherman's troops entered Columbia, South February 17, 1865.

Facing Sherman in this region was a Confederate army under Beauregard. He had nowhere near enough men to deal with Sherman, forcing him to abandon Charleston and Wilmington. Beauregard seemed to have lost the ability to fight and Lee replaced him with General Joseph E. Johnston on February 23. The Confederates tried to harass Sherman as best they could, but they were fighting a losing battle. There were fights, but most of them were merely large skirmishes.

Sherman arrived in Fayetteville on March 11 and established communication with Union forces operating further north. Johnston was still determined to stop Sherman, attempting to oppose him 4 miles (6km) from Bentonville on March 19. The initial Confederate attack was successful, but by the afternoon Sherman had significantly reinforced his front line

OPPOSITE ABOVE: Company K, 3rd Regiment, Massachusetts Heavy Artillery at Fort Stevens, District of Columbia.

OPPOSITE BELOW: General George Custer.

ABOVE RIGHT: Ruins of the Franklin Courthouse at Chambersburg, Pennsylvania, destroyed by Confederate forces in 1864.

RIGHT: General Sherman near Atlanta, Georgia, in 1864.

and Johnston realized that the game was up and that he faced being surrounded. Johnston had been able to amass only some 14,000 men and while casualties were relatively even, over 600 Confederates were taken prisoner.

Sherman reached Goldsboro on March 23, by which stage his army had marched 425 miles (684km) from Savannah, over the worst possible terrain, and had crossed five rivers.

Things had not gone well for the Confederacy in the North and Richmond had been imperiled. Back in May 1864 Grant had begun his offensive in the

Wilderness and Union troops had moved up the James river. By May 9 Union troops were heading towards Petersburg, though Richmond was the ultimate goal. What had really changed the course of the campaign in Virginia was the realization on Grant's part that he could not dislodge Lee from his entrenchments to the north of the James river. Grant decided he would have to try to get behind Lee and cut him off from his supplies, and proposed to move to the south side of the James river.

There was a vicious fight at Piedmont, near Staunton, on June 5, 1864 and another at Lynchburg between June 17 and

18. What has always remained an unanswered question is why Lee did not stop, or at least challenge Grant, when he crossed the Chickahominy and James rivers. Some believe this failure was even worse than that of Gettysburg.

By early June Union forces were testing the defenses at Petersburg, which had been hastily manned. After Richmond,

ABOVE: The Battle of Winchester, fought in the Shenandoah Valley.

OPPOSITE: Map of the Battle of Nashville, December 15–16, 1864.

Petersburg was the most important Confederate center in Virginia. Beauregard commanded the Confederates and realized he had insufficient troops. Petersburg, just 23 miles (37km) from Richmond, had a population of 18,000, and was built on the south bank of the Appomattox river. The problem for the Confederates was that Grant's troops were north of the James river, and were presenting as much of a threat to Lee as the Union troops, that were threatening Petersburg, were to Beauregard.

Grant believed that Petersburg could be taken relatively easily and ordered troops to move up from Bermuda Hundred to Petersburg on June 15, with orders to take Petersburg as quickly as possible. The troops, under General Smith, amounted to some 16,000 and Beauregard had just 5,400 men. For some bizarre reason Smith failed to capitalize on the opportunity, which meant that Grant had to lay siege to Petersburg from June 1864 until April 1865.

By June 18 Lee was ordering troops to Petersburg, the vanguard of his army adding 25,000 men to the defense, and by lunchtime Lee was there himself. In the attacks on Petersburg, between June 15 and 18, Union losses amounted to some 10,000 men, but Lee was now dug in along a 25-mile (40-km) front, covering Richmond

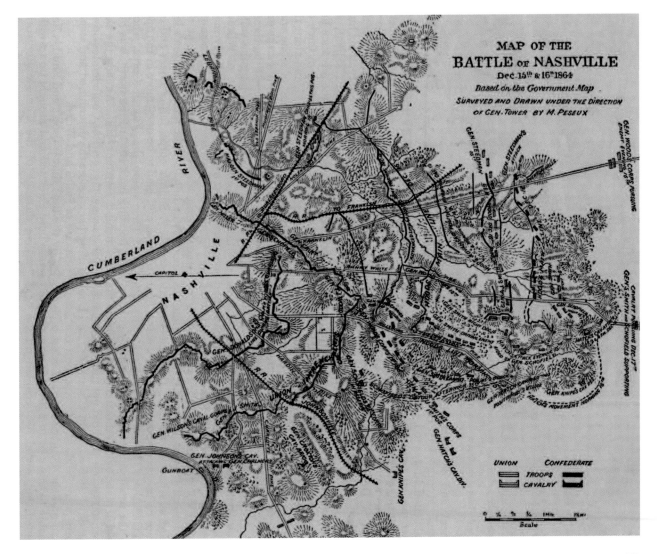

MAP OF THE
BATTLE OF NASHVILLE
Dec. 15th & 16th 1864
Based on the Government Map
SURVEYED AND DRAWN UNDER THE DIRECTION
OF GEN. TOWER BY M. PESEUX

and Petersburg from White Oak Swamp to Jerusalem Plank Road.

The actual assaults on the Confederate lines took place on June 17 and 18, primarily by troops under the command of General Burnside. Central to this engagement was what became known as the Battle of the Crater. Union engineers had excavated a tunnel over 500 feet (150m) long, extending directly under the Confederate fortifications. Some 8,000 pounds (3630kg) of gunpowder was dragged into the tunnel and was detonated at 1645 on July 30, 1864, causing a huge blast and blowing a vast hole, some 30 feet deep, 60 feet wide and 170 feet long (9 x 18 x 50m) in the Confederate defenses. Union troops were then pushed into the crater to

take advantage of the Confederate shock, resulting in costly hand-to-hand fighting and Union losses that amounted to nearly 4,000 men. The finger of blame was pointed at Burnside, who was removed from his command.

On August 18, 1864 Union troops tried to destroy the Weldon Railroad, which led to a violent confrontation costing the lives of over 4,000 Union troops. The railroad was again attacked from August 22 to 24, leading to a further engagement on August 25.

The final offensive of the Confederates at Petersburg took place on March 25, 1865, when Lee ordered an attack on Fort Stedman on Hare's Hill and 10,000 Confederates, under Major General Gordon, stormed the fort and captured several batteries of artillery. Union troops were ordered to counter-attack, and led by the 200th Pennsylvania, they took the fort in 20 minutes at a cost of 122 men. Other Pennsylvanian units overran the captured batteries and 1,600 Confederates were captured.

OPPOSITE: ABOVE: Hospital for Federal soldiers, Nashville, Tennessee, 1864.

OPPOSITE BELOW: The Federal outer line, Nashville, on December 16, 1864.

ABOVE RIGHT: Ruins of a rail depot left by Sherman's men.

RIGHT: A crippled locomotive of the Richmond & Petersburg Railroad, destroyed by the Federal Army in 1865.

ending the war. But Grant and Lee were military men and not politicians and it would be left to others to make the decisions. On April 7, 1865 Grant invited the surrender of Lee's army. He had reached Farmville and wrote to Lee: "The result of last week must convince you of the hopelessness of further resistance on the part of the Army of Northern Virginia in this struggle. I feel that it is so, and regard it as my duty to shift from myself the responsibility of any further effusion of blood, by asking of you the surrender of that portion of the Confederate army known as the Army of Northern Virginia."

Lee's reply was not exactly as Grant had hoped. Lee did not regard the situation as hopeless, but he was unwilling for more blood to be uselessly shed and

It had become increasingly obvious that there was nothing Lee could do to stop Grant's army from linking up with Sherman's forces. There was another disaster at Five Forks, Virginia, on April 1, when Sheridan destroyed a Confederate force under Major General Pickett. Sheridan also destroyed railroads, mills, and factories around Charlottesville and then, at the head of 10,000 cavalry, headed for the White House, having taken 4,500 prisoners.

On the morning of April 2, 1865 Lee was sure he had to abandon Petersburg and retreat towards Richmond, it being only a matter of time before Grant overran the Petersburg defenses.

Grant and Lee had already met while serving in Mexico. Early in March 1865 Lee approached Grant with a view to

wanted to know what the conditions of surrender might be.

Grant informed Lee that terms could be discussed, yet Lee was still not sure if the situation was as desperate as it seemed. By April 8, while Lee's army was resting to the east of Appomattox Courthouse, Lee proposed to see if Grant was blocking escape routes, and if he was, then there would be no option but to surrender.

Custer's cavalry made a dash to destroy the railroad to the west of Appomattox Station, but was attacked by Confederate troops at dawn the following day. As he fell back, however, more Union troops moved up in support. Lee and Grant determined to meet and discuss the terms of surrender. To this end, a Union officer would lead Lee to the village of Appomattox Courthouse, where he would meet with Grant in a house owned by Wilmer McLean. Grant arrived shortly after 1:00pm on April 9. His terms were: "The officers and men surrendered to be paroled and disqualified from taking up arms again until properly exchanged and all arms, ammunition, and supplies to be delivered up as captured property."

OPPOSITE ABOVE: View of the James river and Kanawah Canal near the Haxall Flour Mills, with the ruins of the Galego Mills beyond, 1865.

OPPOSITE BELOW: The monitor USS *Onondaga* on the James river in 1864, with soldiers rowing ashore in the foreground.

RIGHT: Appomattox Courthouse.

Research Projects

Explain and summarize the Battle of Lookout Mountain.

Lee knew he had no choice. The two men talked for a while after signing, and at 1600 Lee left, the two meeting again the following morning. The official surrender of the troops took place on April 12, with Confederate regiments arriving at a field near Appomattox Courthouse, where they stacked their arms and colors. Some 26,018 men surrendered and were then paroled.

Meanwhile, Sherman was pushing towards Raleigh in North Carolina, when he heard about the surrender at Appomattox. It was April 13 and the inhabitants of Raleigh ran towards his

troops carrying white flags. Elements of his cavalry were at Greensboro and others near Columbus and Macon, Georgia, and Sherman was intending to cut off General Johnston's retreat.

The following day, the Union received a note from Johnston to Sherman, proposing a temporary truce. They agreed to meet near Durham Station on April 17 but, as Sherman was about to get on the train, he received word that Lincoln had been assassinated. Sherman went ahead with the meeting and learned that Johnston was prepared to surrender his troops once

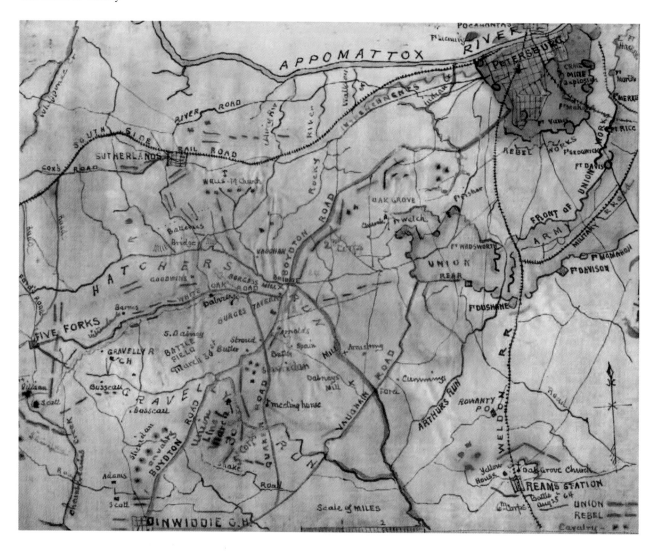

he had received permission from the Confederate President Davis. They met again the following day, when haggling took place.

Under the terms of Lincoln's Proclamation of Amnesty of December 8, 1863, any Confederate below the rank of colonel would be given an immediate pardon. Grant had extended that pardon to all officers, including Lee himself, and Johnston was keen for a similar bargain to

be struck. One of the sticking points, however, was John C. Breckinridge, who was the Confederate Secretary of War, but had also been the Vice President of the United States. The only advice Sherman could give Johnston where Breckinridge was concerned was that he should leave the country and never return.

An outline agreement was ready for presentation to Washington on April 18. Washington wanted terms no better nor

ABOVE: Plan of the Battle of Five Forks, March 31–April 1, 1865.

OPPOSITE: Soldiers on the banks of the Appomattox river at Johnson's Mill.

worse than the ones Lee had been forced to sign. Johnston had no choice and the terms were signed on April 26.

The total number of men involved in Johnston's agreement was 89,270. There were, of course, isolated commands that did not surrender at this stage. In fact there was another major engagement in Texas as late as mid-May 1865. The battle took place between May 12 and 13 and ended in a victory for the Confederacy. As the former Confederate President Jefferson Davis wrote in his memoirs: "Though very small in comparison to its great battles, [Palmito Ranch] deserves notice as having closed the long struggle as it opened, with a Confederate victory."

Text-Dependent Questions

1. When General Buell took control of the Army of Ohio, where was his first target?

2. What was Pierre Gustave Toutant Beauregard's nickname?

3. When did the surrender by Confederate army general Robert E. Lee take place?

Chapter Two
CASUALTIES OF WAR

When Abraham Lincoln was inaugurated for the second time on March 4, 1865 the war was nearly over. The conflict had actually cost far more than would have been needed to buy the freedom of each individual slave in the South. Only five days after the surrender of Lee's Army of Northern Virginia, Abraham Lincoln, like thousands of other Americans during the American Civil War, met a violent end at the hands of a man with a gun.

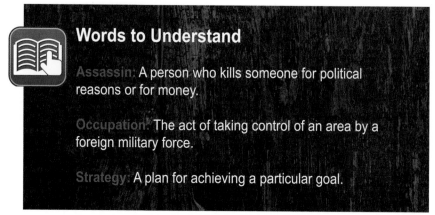

Words to Understand

Assassin: A person who kills someone for political reasons or for money.

Occupation: The act of taking control of an area by a foreign military force.

Strategy: A plan for achieving a particular goal.

JOHN WILKES BOOTH (1838–65)

John Wilkes Booth was born on May 10, 1838 to parents both in the theatrical profession who moved to the United States from England. Like his parents, Booth also went into the acting profession. He was a Confederate sympathizer, and strongly opposed to abolition. Lincoln represented everything Booth hated

most, and he took his chance to strike at the man he saw as responsible for the downfall of the South. Aided by his co-conspirators Booth assassinated President Abraham Lincoln at Ford's Theater in Washington, D.C. on April 14, 1865. At 10:00pm, halfway through the final act, Booth slipped into the corridor behind the presidential box, opened the door, and shot Lincoln. Unfortunately for Lincoln, Booth was successful in carrying out the plot. Lincoln was assassinated by one shot to the back of the head, a wound that proved fatal, for he died the following day. After the assassination Booth fled to southern Maryland and then to Virginia. He was finally tracked down at a farm where he was hiding in a barn. The barn was subsequently set on fire when movement was seen in the building. Booth was located and shot by Boston Corbett, a Union soldier. Booth's companion gave himself up. Eight other conspirators or suspects were hunted down, tried and convicted, and four were hanged shortly thereafter.

Booth's body was eventually taken to Washington Navy Yard for identification and autopsy. He was buried in his family's plot at Green Mount Cemetery, Baltimore.

Lincoln had been due to attend a performance of Our American Cousin at Ford's Theater in Washington on the night of April 14, 1865. He arrived with his wife and guests at 8:30pm, but at 10:00pm, halfway through the final act, an assassin slipped into the corridor behind the presidential box, opened the door, and shot Lincoln through the head. Lincoln was mortally wounded and died of his injuries at 7:22am the next day.

The killer was a Southerner, an actor by the name of John Wilkes Booth. Lincoln represented everything Booth hated most, and he took his chance to strike at the man he saw as responsible for the downfall of the South. Booth was tracked down to a barn in Virginia, which was set on fire. Someone saw him moving

OPPOSITE: The assassination of President Lincoln, at Ford's Theater, Washington D.C. on April 14, 1865.

ABOVE: President Lincoln.

within the building, and shot at him, and Booth staggered out and died.

For a country such as the United States, barely a century old and still expanding, the Civil War had involved vast numbers of men. In July 1861 the Union army had been able to muster some 187,000 men, compared with the Confederacy's 112,000. By 1865 the

Union army had increased to nearly a million (up to 50,000 in the U.S. Navy) and the Confederate armies could boast 450,000 men.

Battlefield casualties had been severe, with major battles involving up to 100,000 Union troops and 60,000 Confederates. In all, some 110,000 Union troops were killed in the field or died of

their wounds, compared with around 90,000 Confederate casualties.

Disease took even more soldiers: an estimated 360,000 Union and 260,000 Confederates died of malaria, typhoid, and dysentery, or as a direct result of their wounds. It has been estimated that the American Civil War cost the United States $20 billion, a huge sum of money, but the cost in human lives was, of course, far more devastating and affected families in all sections of American society. Lincoln's own wife lost three brothers fighting for the Confederacy, and his sister-in-law was the widow of the Confederate officer, Benjamin Helm, who died at Chickamauga.

Family links such as these prompted heated debates and accusations after the war, while associates of Lincoln's assassin, Booth, had death penalties imposed. Indeed some of them were implicated in a

failed plot to assassinate the Secretary of State, William Seward, to coincide with the murder of Abraham Lincoln.

Further accusations were leveled at John C. Breckinridge, who had been President James Buchanan's vice president, in that he had been part of a pre-war

Southern conspiracy to derail the Union. Even Lincoln was accused of having pro-slavery leanings, having come from Kentucky, a slave state, though any suggestions that Lincoln may have favored the South were dispelled when he was murdered.

Though some suspected a major Southern conspiracy behind the assassination of Lincoln, in fact there was

ABOVE: The 3rd Connecticut Infantry at Camp Douglas, 1861.

LEFT: James Buchanan.

OPPOSITE ABOVE: Company G of the 114th pensylvania Infantry at Petersburg, Virginia.

OPPOSITE: The 93rd New York Infantry at Antietam.

none. None of the Confederate leaders had any idea that Booth had been planning to assassinate the president. Had the killing taken place much earlier, before Antietam and the subsequent Emancipation Proclamation, the resolve of the South may have been called into question.

On paper, at least, the war should never have lasted so long, nor should there have been so many casualties. In many respects the style of government in the South had been instrumental in allowing the Confederates to be more flexible and to reward their more superior commanders with swift promotion. By the end of the war the South had 17 lieutenant generals and eight full generals, giving them far better chains of command.

The North, on the other hand, frequently allowed overbearing and overcautious politicians to interfere with

the running of the Union army, while the seemingly overwhelming strength of the Army of the Potomac was held back by a string of poor appointments. McClellan led the army twice and Washington tried to make it a force to be reckoned with, using McDowell, Pope, Burnside, Hooker, and Meade to achieve this aim. At various times the vast army moved at a snail's pace, barely able to defend itself, while at others its strength was dissipated as it blundered forward with reckless abandon.

Militarily, the principal difference between the North and the South was the way in which the armies had been led. To begin with, perhaps, the Southern troops had had the edge, but as the war progressed the Union troops were better trained and began to equal them on the battlefield. On both sides, officer casualties were disproportionately large, in that aggressive commanders at company, regimental level, and above had to lead their men from the front.

Despite the huge numbers under arms, many of the troops in the early years were volunteers and thousands sought to evade conscription, while thousands more fled when faced with a determined enemy. The penalty for desertion, for both Union and Confederate soldiers, was death, but this rarely needed to be carried out. This was because men were prepared to suffer within the bosom of their regiment, rather than face life outside it, and were willing to cope with deprivation and danger on the battlefield as long as they had faith in their

officers. Here the Confederates scored well: often up against a numerically superior foe, they fought the larger Union armies to a standstill.

As the war progressed, the Southern troops had to accept that their own homes and land were under **occupation** or threat by Union troops. It is testament to their resolve that they stayed with the main field armies and did not desert to protect their own property. Both sides were facing what appeared to be an indifferent civilian population and even worse were the men who had avoided conscription and were making fat profits from the war behind the lines. In fact, profits could be made on both sides of the front line and even at the height of the Union blockades, only half the blockade-runners were intercepted by the Union navy. This meant that expensive imported products, if they could be obtained, would find a ready market anywhere a speculator chose to offer them.

There are many issues to ponder when the American Civil War is examined in detail. First and foremost there was the balance of manpower and resources, where the Union always had a distinct advantage. Nevertheless, it has been asked on many occasions why it took four years to crush the

Confederacy, when it was so woefully weaker than the Union. The first answer relates directly to the use of available resources, in that to begin with, the Union was simply wasteful, while the South put its manpower and resources to direct and practical use. The second is the leadership of the military. Again, as we have seen, the Union armies fluctuated from being timid to aggressive, according to the commander who was in charge at the time.

The South certainly had the upper hand, at least until Antietam, and probably beyond. It so nearly won the key battle at Gettysburg, which would have led to the destruction of the main Union force of the

Army of the Potomac, and would have left much of the North, including Washington, at its mercy. Considering the relatively short distance between Richmond and Washington, it is also a wonder why neither capital fell sooner; Richmond, however, did ultimately fall towards the end of the war. In fact the majority of the battles were fought over a relatively small area of the United States, principally in the East, and Virginia can claim the dubious honor of hosting more battles during the Civil War than any other state.

Had key Union commanders, such as Grant, Sheridan and Sherman, come to the fore earlier and had been given full rein to

OPPOSITE ABOVE: Men of the Irish-American 9th Massachusetts Infantry, near Washington, D.C.

OPPOSITE BELOW: Depot of the 17th New York Artillery.

ABOVE: Soldiers' graves at City Point, Virginia.

Research Projects

What was it like being a soldier in the Civil War? How were ill and injured soldiers looked after? How long did it take for the South to recover economically for it was the war's battlefield?

Text-Dependent Questions

1. Who assassinated Lincoln?

2. How many battlefield casualties were there?

3. How many soldiers died from disease or from their wounds?

prosecute their versions of total war, even Lee could not have stood in their way in achieving a quick and effective victory.

For both sides, the key to victory had always been the use of strategy and communications, coupled with effective logistics. The Confederacy quite rightly adopted a defensive **strategy**, fighting on its own ground so that communications and resupply were the more effective. For the Union it was an offensive war, in that it was necessary to forge a way into the South, seize land and population centers and keep them. The South, after all, was hostile territory, so as more of it began to fall, more Union troops could be diverted to the mundane task of occupation.

Their individual strategical approaches reflect the difference in aspirations of the Confederacy and the Union. At no time did the Confederacy seriously wish to impose its government on the North, but as far as the Union was concerned, it was the exact opposite; it did wish to impose its will on the South and this was what dictated the offensive and defensive strategies used by the two sides.

Once Union troops had begun to occupy the South, the Confederacy had to rely on mobile armies, which could cut into the occupation zones and seize weapons, ammunition, food, and horses from the invading Union troops. This strategy worked extremely well for a long time and Confederate soldiers were able to rely on the Union army to supply them, often with food and goods they had not seen for months, as a result of their ill-defended supply centers.

The Confederates did, of course, do far more than simply counter-attack the weak points of the Union front line. In 1863 Lee launched a massive raid into the North, with the objective of harassing Northern civilians and, of course, drawing out an ill-prepared Union army that could be defeated in a decisive manner on the battlefield.

Both sides should have realized that the way in which the war was being fought had direct parallels with the American Revolution, when it was the British who seized the ground and established garrisons, only to find themselves vulnerable because they had not cornered Washington's army and destroyed it. For several months this was exactly the predicament in which the Union army found itself, while facing an aggressive and elusive Robert E. Lee.

Both the Confederates and the Union were obsessed with taking the other's capitals and defending their own. False alarms at various times led to thousands of Union troops being diverted to holding the approaches to Washington, while on other occasions, vast Union armies that could have done far more harm to the Confederacy, fruitlessly sat around Richmond or battered themselves to a standstill against the capital's defenses.

The South was ultimately doomed, not when Richmond came under threat, but when the Union forces gained control of the Mississippi Valley. Sherman's 2,000-mile (3220-km) rampage through Georgia and the Carolinas wrecked the South's infrastructure and proved once and for all that the Confederate armies were incapable of stopping a determined Union force.

Towards the end of the war there were fewer set-piece battles, it being more a question of the two armies being in continual contact with one another. They would clash when one army advanced too quickly or when one was too tardy in retreat. This remorseless form of warfare, with no peace, no time for rest or recuperation, could only have one victor: the Union. It is true to say that the South never did receive a mortal blow, but died the death of a thousand cuts.

To reiterate, the American Civil War was fought not to end slavery but to preserve the Union. Rightly or wrongly, the Southern states, seizing on a technicality in the constitutional agreements, effectively withdrew from the Union, and everything that happened from this point on was either in defense of their right to secede or to prevent the Union from making them change their minds.

But perhaps this was not the whole story. As Lincoln himself confessed at his second inaugural address: "All knew that this interest [Southern slavery] was, somehow, the cause of this war."

If this is what Lincoln really believed, then we return to the question, why did he not bow to the abolitionists earlier? Possibly the preservation of the Union just tipped the balance; Lincoln had written to Frederick Douglass that he would emancipate all, some or none of the slaves to achieve this aim.

In the post-war period, many commentators and historians tried to get to the root of the causes and effects of the American Civil War. To some, the war was a matter of economics, the North wishing to bring the South fully into its economic empire and crush, once and for all, any notion of independence, while others claim the war had been totally avoidable. Some thought the North, and Lincoln in particular, had given in too easily to the demands of abolitionist extremists and that it was the inherent threat of emancipation that had forced the secession of the South. But other kinds of extremists had been active in the South; they had a vested interest in preserving slavery, and by pressing their case they had forced the South to take the ultimate step.

The time following the Civil War was known as the Reconstruction Period, when infrastructure was rebuilt, the North and South were redefined, and efforts were made to bring a greater degree of homogeneity to the United States.

The South, the war's battlefield and the center of slavery, struggled to come to terms with defeat and suffered even more during the post-war years. Economically, it fell even further behind the North and the disparity in wealth and population increased. The South fell prey to speculators able to make rich profits at the expense of Southern landowners. The cotton industry did recover, but this time it was operated using paid workers. Post-war, Great Britain, for example, was now importing far more Southern cotton than it had before the conflict.

As for the former slaves, their long journey towards truly equal rights would have to continue until it became an unstoppable force 90 years later. As for Lincoln, he had once said that there could be no regrets about the war, in that it would provide the necessary conditions for "A just, and a lasting peace."

BELOW: The Jefferson Memorial, Washington D.C.

TIME LINE OF THE CIVIL WAR

1860

November 6
Abraham Lincoln elected president.

December 20
South Carolina secedes from the Union, followed two months later by other states.

1861

February 9
Jefferson Davis becomes the first and only President of the Confederate States of America.

March 4
Lincoln sworn in as 16th President of the United States.

April 12
Confederates, under Beauregard, open fire on Fort Sumter at Charleston, South Carolina.

April 15
Lincoln issues a proclamation calling for 75,000 volunteers.

April 17
Virginia secedes from the Union, followed by three other states, making an 11-state Confederacy.

April 19
Blockade proclamation issued by Lincoln.

April 20
Robert E. Lee resigns his command in the United States Army.

July 4
Congress authorizes a call for half a million volunteers.

July 21
Union forces, under McDowell, defeated at Bull Run.

July 27
McClellan replaces McDowell.

November 1
McClellan becomes general-in-chief of Union forces after the resignation of Winfield Scott.

November 8
Two Confederate officials are seized en route to Great Britain by the Union navy.

1862

February 6
Grant captures Fort Henry in Tennessee.

March 8–9
The Confederate ironclad *Merrimac* sinks two Union warships, then fights the *Monitor*.

April 6–7
Confederates attack Grant at Shiloh on the Tennessee river.

April 24
Union ships under Farragut take New Orleans.

May 31
Battle of Seven Pines, where Joseph E. Johnston is badly wounded when he nearly defeats McClellan's army.

June 1
Robert E. Lee takes over from Johnston and renames the force the Army of Northern Virginia.

June 25–July 1
Lee attacks McClellan near Richmond during the Seven Days' Battles. McClellan retreats towards Washington.

July 11
Henry Halleck becomes general -in-chief of the Union army.

August 29–30
Union army, under Pope, defeated by Jackson and Longstreet at the Second Battle of Bull Run.

September 4–9
Lee invades the North, pursued by McClellan's Union army.

September 17
Battle of Antietam. Both sides are badly mauled. Lee withdraws to Virginia.

September 22
Preliminary Emancipation Proclamation issued by Lincoln.

November 7
McClellan replaced by Burnside as commander of the Army of the Potomac.

December 13
Burnside decisively defeated at Fredericksburg, Virginia, 1863.

1863

January 1
Lincoln issues the final Emancipation Proclamation.

January 29
Grant assumes command of the Army of the West.

March 3
U.S. Congress authorizes conscription.

May 1–4
Hooker is decisively defeated by Lee at the Battle of Chancellorsville. Stonewall Jackson is mortally wounded.

June 3
Lee invades the North, heading into Pennsylvania.

June 28
George Meade replaces Hooker as commander of the Army of the Potomac.

July 1–3
Lee is defeated at the Battle of Gettysburg.

July 4
Vicksburg – the last Confederate stronghold on the Mississippi – falls to Grant and the Confederacy is now split in two.

July 13–16
Draft riots in New York

July 18
54th Massachusetts, under Shaw, fails in its assault against Fort Wagner, South Carolina.

August 21
Quantrill's raiders murder the inhabitants of Lawrence, Kansas

September 19–20
Bragg's Confederate Army of Tennessee defeats General Rosecrans at Chickamauga.

October 16
Grant given command of all operations in the West.

November 19
Lincoln gives his famous Gettysburg Address.

November 23–25
Grant defeats Bragg at Chattanooga.

1864

March 9
Grant assumes command of all armies of the Union. Sherman takes Grant's old job as commander in the West.

May 5–6
Battle of the Wilderness.

May 8–12
Battle of Spotsylvania.

June 1–3
Battle of Cold Harbor.

June 15
Union troops miss a chance to capture Petersburg.

July 20
Sherman defeats Hood at Atlanta.

August 29
Former General McClellan becomes the Democratic nominee for president.

September 2
Atlanta is captured by Sherman.

October 19
Sheridan defeats Early's Confederates in the Shenandoah Valley.

November 8
Lincoln is re-elected president.

November 15
Sherman begins his March to the Sea.

December 15–16
Hood is defeated at the Battle of Nashville.

December 21 Sherman reached Savannah in Georgia.

1865

January 31
Thirteenth amendment approved to abolish slavery.

February 3
Peace conference between Lincoln and Confederate vice president fails at Hampton Roads, Virginia.

March 4
Lincoln inaugurated as president.

March 25
Lee's last offensive is defeated after four hours at Petersburg.

April 2
Grant pushes through Lee's defensive lines at Petersburg. Richmond is evacuated as Union troops enter.

April 4
Lincoln tours Richmond.

April 9
Lee surrenders his army to Grant at Appomattox Courthouse, Virginia.

April 10
Major victory celebrations in Washington.

April 14
Lincoln shot in a Washington theater.

April 15
Lincoln dies and Andrew Johnson becomes president.

April 18
Confederate General Johnston surrenders to Sherman in North Carolina.

April 19
Lincoln's funeral procession.

April 26
Lincoln's assassin, Booth, is shot and dies in Virginia.

May 23–24
Victory parade held in Washington.

December 6
Thirteenth Amendment approved by Congress. It is ratified and slavery is formally abolished.

BELOW: The Lincoln Memorial, Washington D.C.

IN THIS TEMPLE
AS IN THE HEARTS OF THE PEOPLE
FOR WHOM HE SAVED THE UNION
THE MEMORY OF ABRAHAM LINCOLN
IS ENSHRINED FOREVER

Educational Videos about the American Civil War

The Gettysburg Address
A speech by U.S. President Abraham Lincoln, one of the best-known in American history. It was delivered by Lincoln during the American Civil War, on the afternoon of Thursday, November 19, 1863, at the dedication of the Soldiers' National Cemetery in Gettysburg, Pennsylvania.

Everyday Animated Map
A useful video explaining how the Union and Confederate armies gained ground through the various battles.

"Dear Sarah," A Soldier's Farewell to his Wife
A Civil War soldier's heartbreaking farewell letter written before his death at Bull Run.

The War Between the States
Historian Garry Adleman gives an overview of the causes, campaigns, and conclusion of the Civil War.

History, Key Figures, and Battles
A useful, concise dramatized, video explaining the American Civil War.

EXAMPLES OF CONFEDERATE UNIFORMS

Robert E. Lee in his general's uniform

Trooper, Stuart's Cavalry Corps.

Infantry Soldier

Marines

Virginia Cavalry

Louisiana
Tigers

Georgia
Infantry

4th Alabama
Regiment

South
Carolina
Regiment

Engineer

73

EXAMPLES OF UNION (FEDERAL) UNIFORMS

Ulysses S. Grant in his general's uniform

Indiana Regiment

5th New York Volunteers

39th New York Voluntry Infantry Regiment

Iron Brigade of the U.S.

U.S. Marine Corps

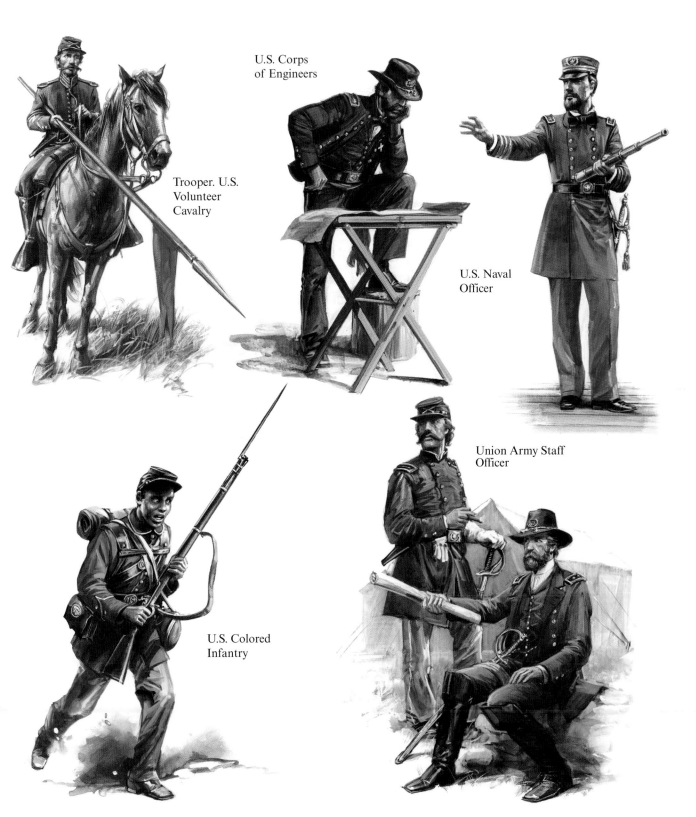

Trooper. U.S. Volunteer Cavalry

U.S. Corps of Engineers

U.S. Naval Officer

Union Army Staff Officer

U.S. Colored Infantry

Series Glossary of Key Terms

Abolitionist A person who wants to eliminate slavery.

Antebellum A term describing the United States before the Civil War.

Artillery Large bore firearms like cannons and mortars.

Assassination A murder for political reasons (usually an important person).

Cash Crop A crop such as cotton, sugar cane, or tobacco sold for cash.

Cavalry A section of the military mounted on horseback.

Confederacy Also called the South or the Confederate States of America. A term given to 11 southern states seceding from the United States in 1860 and 1861.

Copperhead A person in the North who sympathized with the South during the Civil war.

Dixie A nickname given to states in the south-east United States.

Dred Scott Decision A decision made by the Supreme Court that said Congress could not outlaw slavery.

Emancipation An act of setting someone free from slavery.

Gabion A basket filled with rocks and earth used to build fortifications.

Fugitive Slave Law A law passed by Congress in 1850 that stipulated escaped slaves in free states had to be retured to their owners.

Infantry Soldiers that travel and fight on foot.

North The states located in the north of the United States, also called the Union.

Plantation An area of land especially in hot parts of the world where crops such as cotton and tobacco are grown.

Slavery The state of a person who is owned or under the control of another.

Secession Withdrawal from the Federal goverment of the United States.

Sectionalism A tendency to be concerned with local interests and customs ahead of the larger country.

South The states located in the south of the United States, also called the Confederacy.

Union The name given to the states that stayed loyal to the United States.

West Point The United States Military Academy.

Yankee A nickname given for people from the North and Union soldiers.

Further Reading and Internet Resources

WEBSITES

http://www.civilwar.org

http://www.historyplace.com/civilwar

http://www.historynet.com/civil-war

www.britannica.com/event/American-Civil-War

BOOKS

Bruce Catton. *The Centennial History of the Civil War,* Doubleday, 1962. Kindle edition 2013.

Ulysses S. Grant. *The Complete Personal Memoirs of Ulysses S*. Grant Seven Treasures Publications, 2009

James Robertson and Neil Kagan. *The Untold Civil War: Exploring the Human Side of War*. National Geographic, 2011.

If you enjoyed this book take a look at Mason Crest's other war series:

The Vietnam War, World War II, Major U.S. Historical Wars.

Index

In this book, page numbers in **bold italic font** indicate photos or videos.

PHOTOGRAPHIC ACKNOWLEDGEMENTS

All images in this book are supplied by the Library of Congess/public domain and under license from © Shutterstock.com other than the following: Regency House Publishing Limited: 7, 72-73, 74-75.

The content of this book was first published as *CIVIL WAR*.

ABOUT THE AUTHOR

Johnathan Sutherland & Diane Canwell

Together, Diane Canwell and Jonathan Sutherland are the authors of 150 books, and have written extensively about the American Civil War. Both have a particular interest in American history, and its military aspects in particular. Several of their books have attracted prizes and awards, including New York Library's Best of Reference and Book List's Editor's Choice.